HEARTH & HOME

a pattern collection by
Kerin Dimeler-Laurence

Copyright 2013 © Knit Picks

All rights reserved. This book or any portion thereof may not be reproduced or used in any manner whatsoever without the express written permission of the publisher except for the use of brief quotations in a book review.

Printed in the United States of America

Second printing, 2014

ISBN 978-1-62767-016-6

Versa Press, Inc
800-447-7829

www.versapress.com

CONTENTS

Fronds Afghan — 6

Flora Dishcloths — 10

Thistle Potholders — 16

Thistle Kitchen Towels — 20

Dandelion Pillows — 24

Dandelion Runner — 30

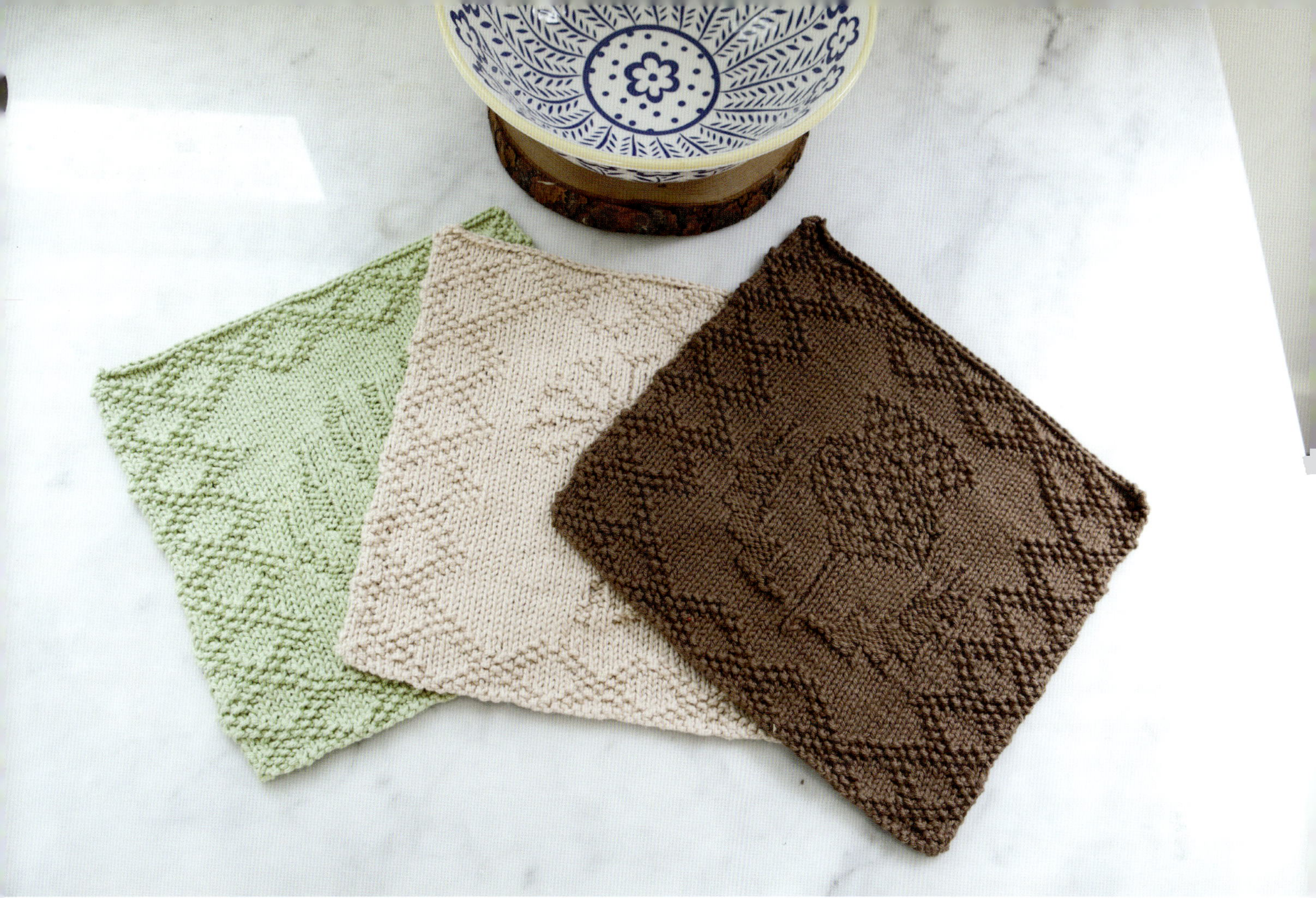

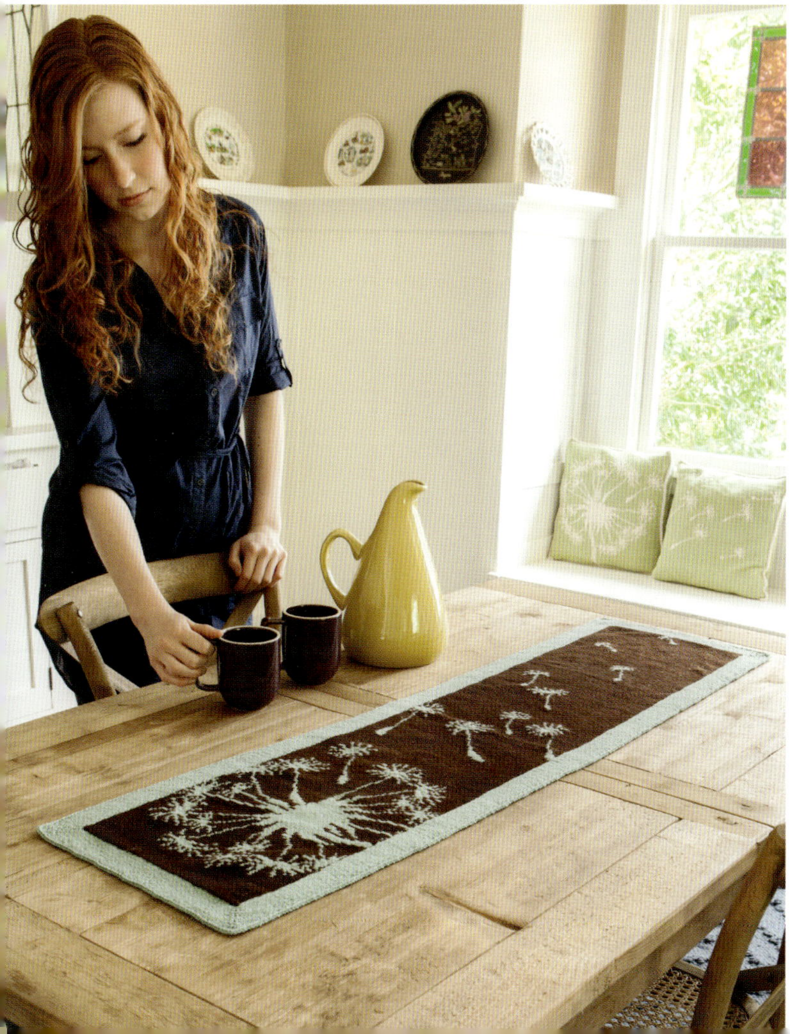

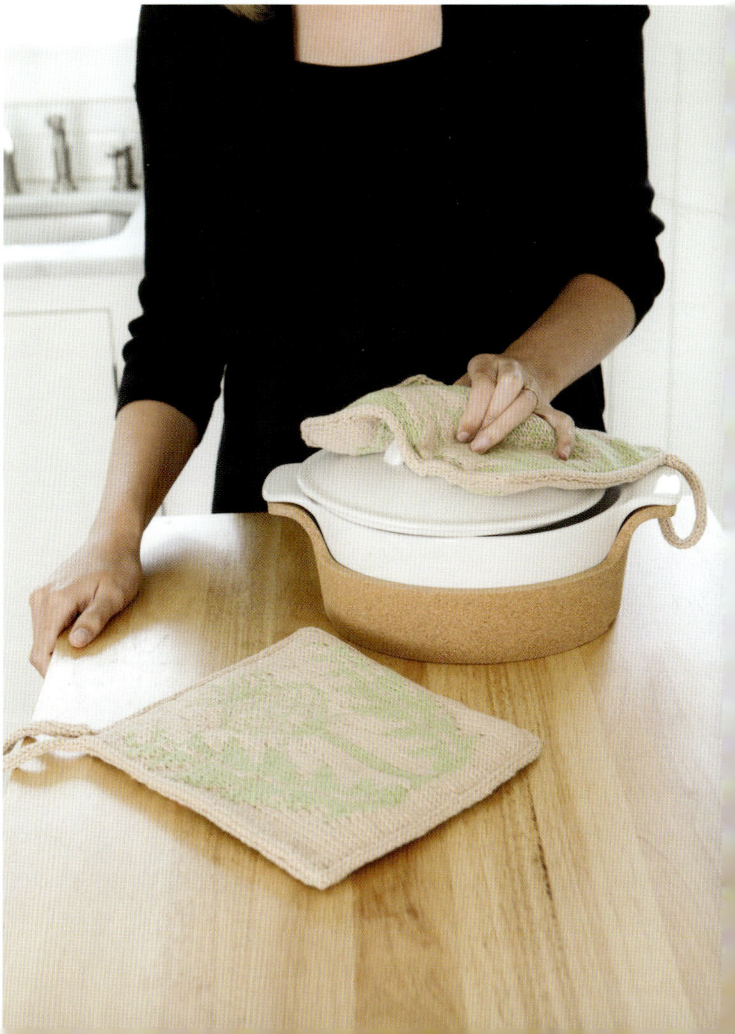

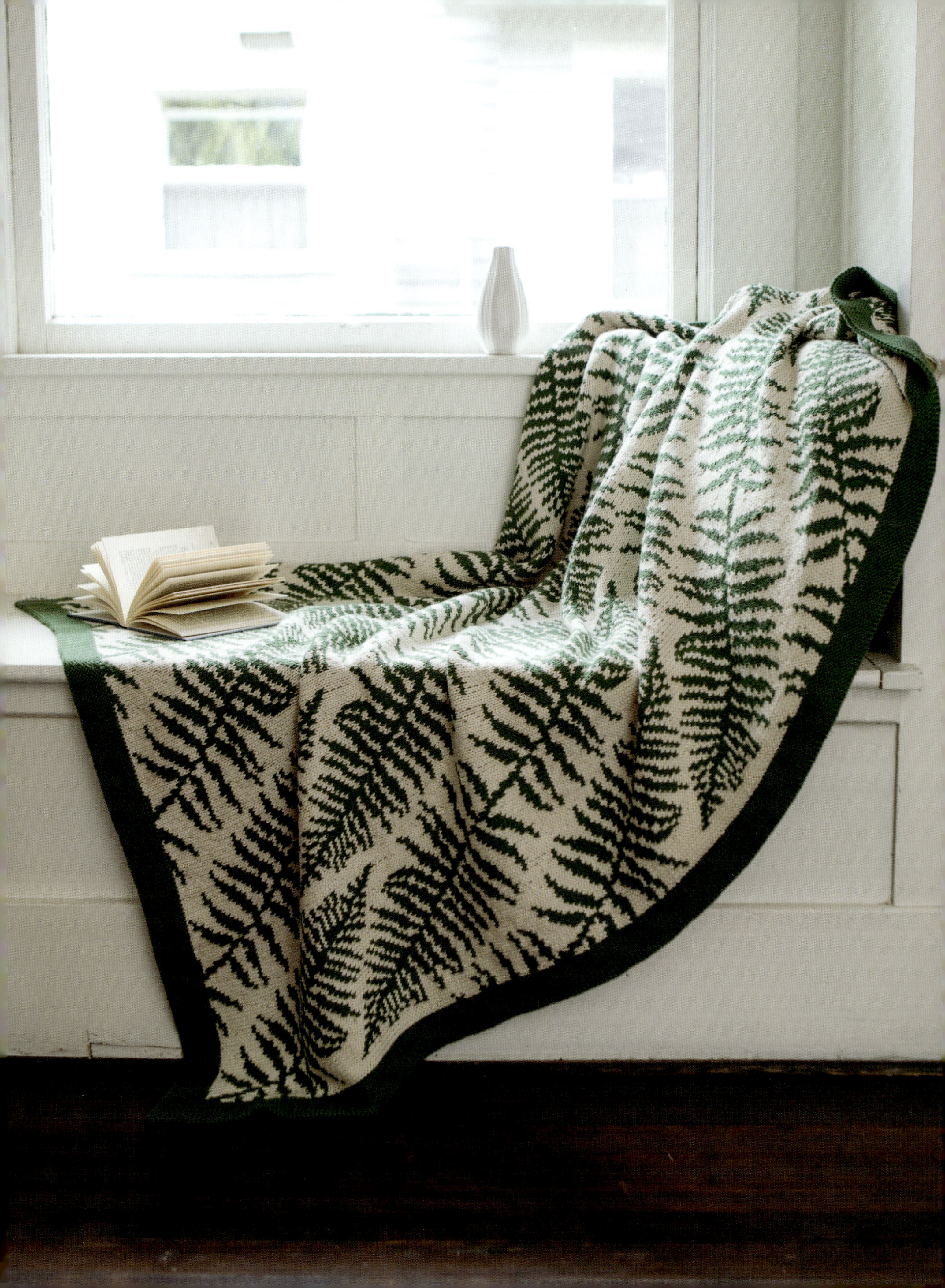

FRONDS AFGHAN

by Kerin Dimeler-Laurence

FINISHED MEASUREMENTS
40x60"

YARN
Knit Picks Comfy Worsted (75% Pima cotton, 25% Acrylic; 109 yards/50g): MC Ivory 24162, 10 balls; CC Jalapeno 24420, 9 balls.

NEEDLES
US 8 (5mm) 24" or longer circular, or size to obtain gauge
24" or longer circular needles one size smaller than those used to obtain gauge

NOTIONS
Tapestry Needle

GAUGE
22 sts and 24 rows = 4" in Stranded St st, blocked.

Fronds Afghan

Notes:
This fanciful afghan is knit flat in Stranded stockinette stitch, with a border picked up and knit on. Be sure to tack down floats of the unused color if it will be running behind five or more stitches of the other color.

DIRECTIONS

With CC and smaller needles, CO 202 sts. Work in Garter st (knit every row) for 19 rows.

On the next row, attach MC and switch to larger needles. The chart is worked over 200 sts; the extra two stitches are a one stitch selvedge on each side for picking up the side borders. Work these stitches in the colors of the adjacent stitch (stitch 1 or 40 of the Fronds chart). Begin working from Fronds Chart from RS row 1, following repeats as shown, between selvedge stitches.

After the last row of the chart, break MC. Switch to smaller needles. With CC, work in Garter st for 19 rows. BO all sts loosely, so that the bound off sts match the stretch of the garter stitch.

Side Borders

Hold the afghan with RS facing. With smaller needles and CC, PU and knit 10 sts up the side of the Garter border, 300 sts up the edge of the Fronds Chart (picking up between selvedge and first charted st) and 10 sts across the other Garter border. Work in Garter st for 18 rows. BO all sts loosely.

Repeat the border on the other side of the afghan.

Finishing

Weave in ends, wash and block to finished measurements. If you wish, line the back of the afghan with a pre-shrunk cotton fabric.

Fronds Chart

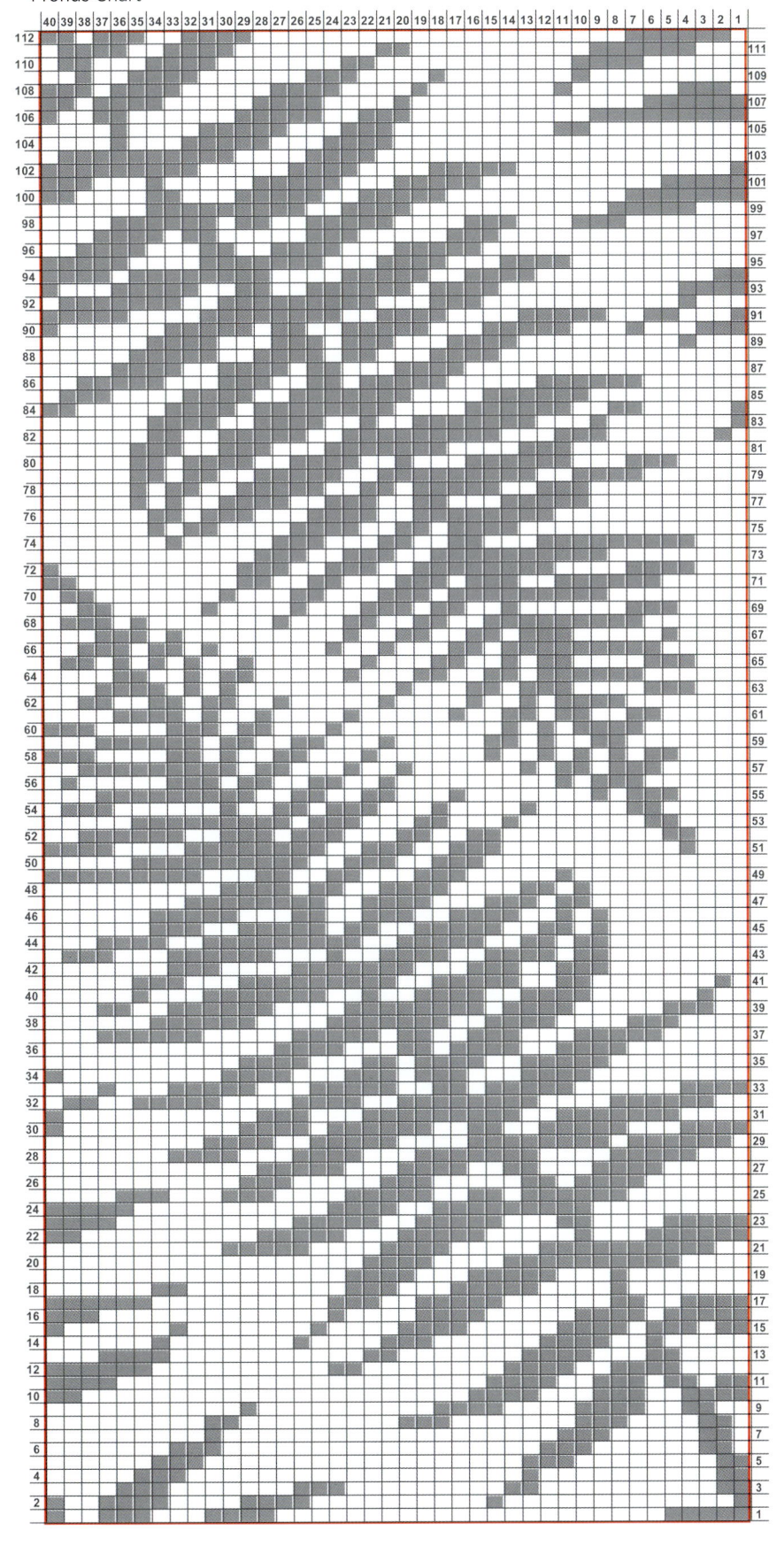

Chart is read from bottom to top. Right side rows are read from right to left, and wrong side rows from left to right.

Work five repeats of the 40 sts of this chart across the body of the afghan, and work three repeats of the 112 rows of the chart. Continue with edging directions.

- ☐ MC Ivory
- ■ CC Jalapeno

Fronds Afghan | 9

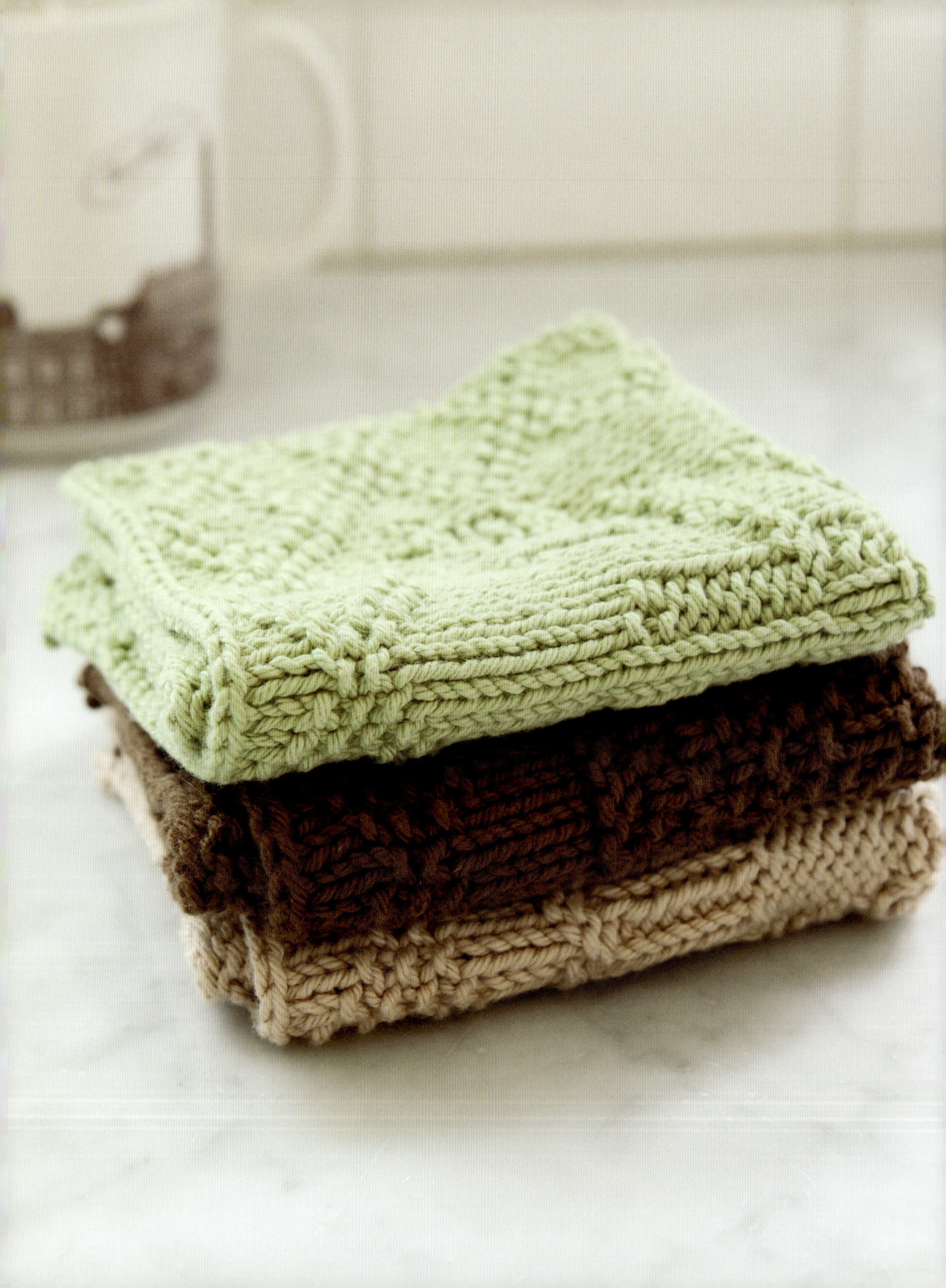

FLORA DISHCLOTHS

by Kerin Dimeler-Laurence

FINISHED MEASUREMENTS
10" square

YARN
Knit Picks Dishie (100% cotton; 190 yards/100g): Linen 25400, Honeydew 25410, Chestnut 25791, 1 ball each.

NEEDLES
US 7 (4.5 mm) straight or circular, or size to obtain gauge

NOTIONS
Tapestry Needle

GAUGE
20 sts and 28 rows = 4" in Brocade (border) pattern, blocked.

Flora Dishcloths

Notes:
A set of three simple dishcloths completes any kitchen.

DIRECTIONS

Each of these cloths is worked the same way, but uses a different color and has a different central motif.

Chestnut: Thistle
Linen: Dandelion
Honeydew: Fern

With specified color, CO 50 sts. Begin working from the chart that goes with that color. After the last charted row, BO all sts.

Finishing

Weave in ends, wash and block to finished measurements.

RS rows are read from right to left, WS rows from left to right.

Legend:

☐ knit
RS: knit stitch
WS: purl stitch

● purl
RS: purl stitch
WS: knit stitch

Thistle

12 | Flora Dishcloths

Dandelion

Fern

14 | Flora Dishcloths

Flora Dishcloths | 15

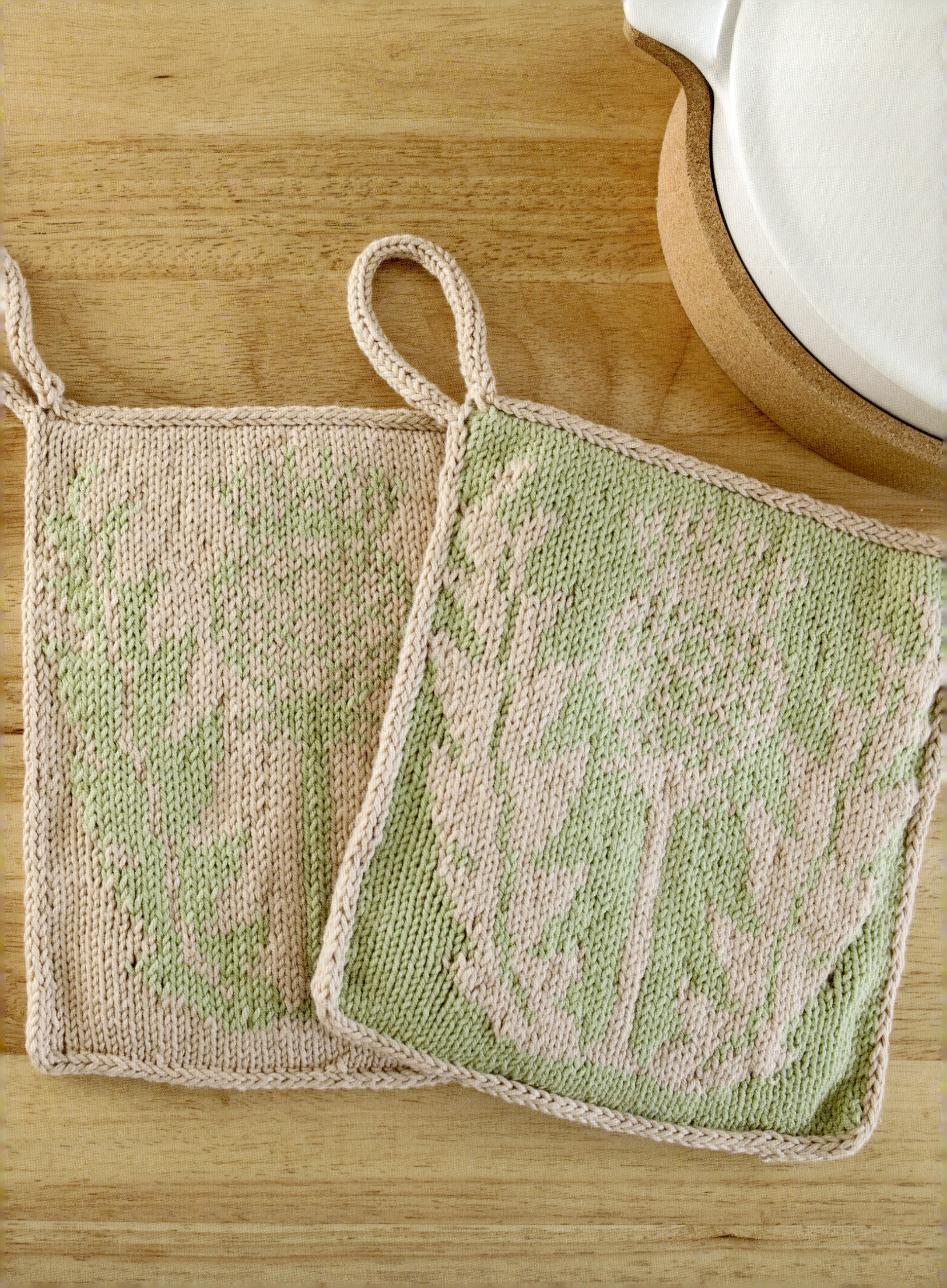

THISTLE POTHOLDERS

by Kerin Dimeler-Laurence

FINISHED MEASUREMENTS
8" square

YARN
Knit Picks Dishie (100% Cotton; 190 yards/100g): Honeydew 25410, Linen 25400, 2 balls each.

NEEDLES
US 6 (4mm) straights or circulars, or size to obtain gauge, plus DPNs for I-cord

NOTIONS
Yarn Needle
Insulating batting such as Insulbrite; 2 pieces each 8" square

GAUGE
22 sts and 31 rows = 4" in Stranded St st, blocked.

Thistle Potholders

The potholders are knit in two sections and then joined together with an applied I-cord border. They are lined with insulating material to keep your hands and surfaces safe!

DIRECTIONS

Each potholder has a Side 1 and Side 2. Make two of each side to make two potholders. With Honeydew (Side 1) or Linen (side 2), CO 44 sts. Begin working from Side 1 or Side 2 chart. Attach the other color when needed, and break it after the last row in which it is used.

After all 62 rows of the chart have been worked, BO all sts loosely in current color.

Using either side as a template, cut a piece of Insulbright batting to go between the two sides.

Fasten off contrasting color yarn ends of both sides; as the wrong sides will not be seen, tying the ends and cutting them short is a quick way to finish these pieces.

I-cord Border

Hold the two sides with their wrong sides together and BO rows on top. With Linen, CO 3 sts onto one DPN and begin I-cord starting at the upper corner:

*Knit two stitches and slip the third stitch knitwise.
PU and knit one stitch through the edge of both sides together.

You will now have 4 stitches on your right needle. Do not turn. Use your left needle tip to pass the slipped stitch over the last knitted stitch. This will leave you with three stitches on your right needle.

Slip these three stitches back onto the left needle tip, or slide to the other end of the needle, purlwise. Tug on the working yarn to tighten up the stitches and pull the working yarn tightly across the back, creating a tube of stitches.

Repeat these steps from * around the potholder, joining the two sides together, until there are only a few inches open on the last side. Insert the Insulbrite batting through the opening and flatten out. Continue the I-cord border until the entire edge has been joined. You will now create a hanging loop.

Hanging Loop

PU and knit one stitch through the edge of both sides together, through the same sts where you began the applied I-cord. You will now have 4 stitches on your right needle. Do not turn.

*Slide the stitches to the opposite end of the DPN. Now the working yarn is at the "wrong" end of your work. Knit the next row, pulling the working yarn tightly across the back of the piece to create a tube.

Repeat from * for 7". Do not BO sts; break yarn, leaving 12" tail. Fold the loop over and graft the live sts of the loop to the CO sts of the applied I-cord.

Weave in ends.

Side 1

Side 2

□ Linen

▨ Honeydew

Charts are followed from bottom to top. RS (odd numbered) rows are read from right to left, and WS (even numbered) rows from left to right. Knit all sts on the RS and purl all sts on the WS.

Thistle Potholders | 19

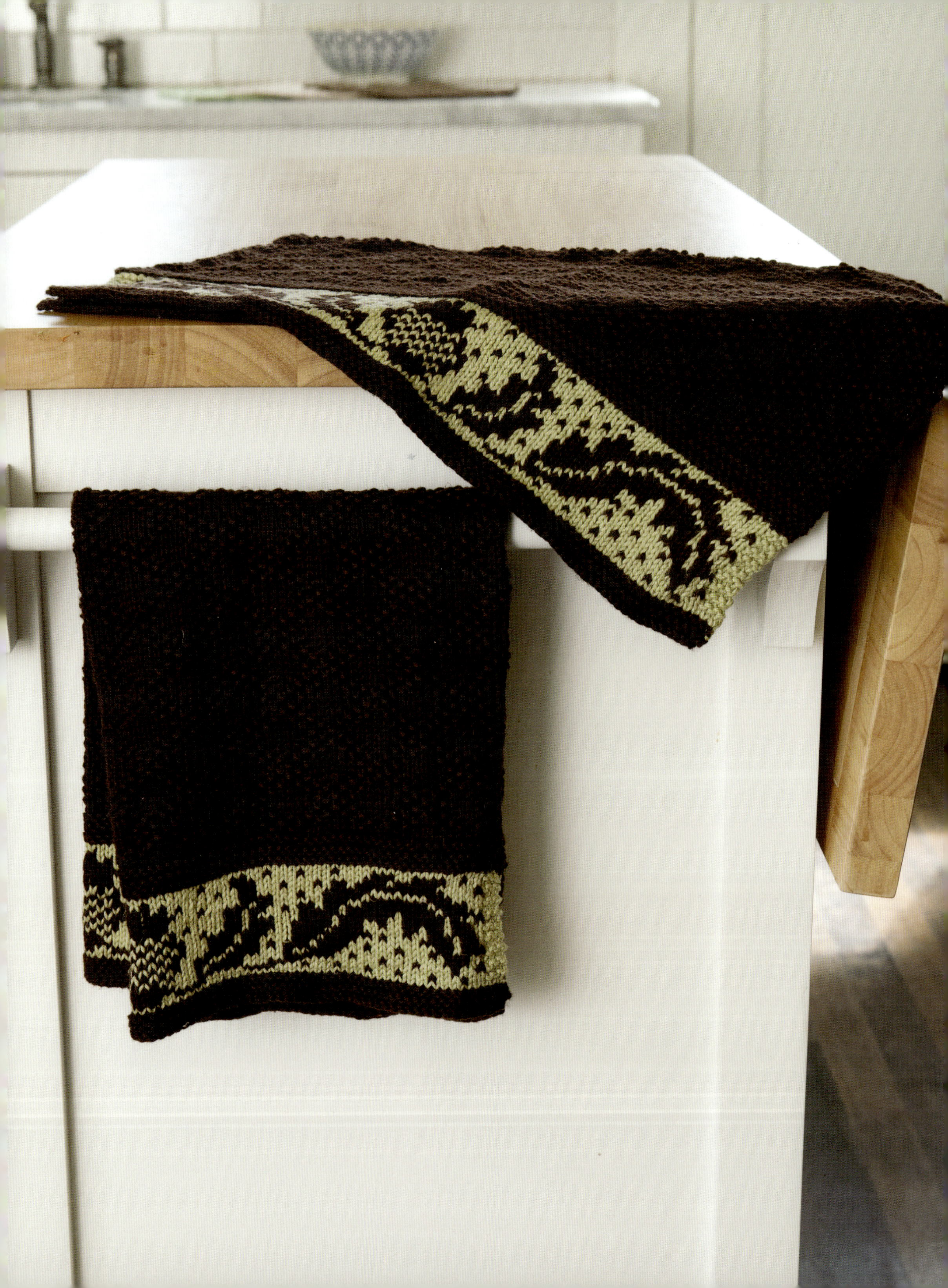

THISTLE KITCHEN TOWELS

by Kerin Dimeler-Laurence

FINISHED MEASUREMENTS
14x22"

YARN
Knit Picks Cotlin (70% Tanguis Cotton, 30% Linen; 123 yards/50g): MC Coffee 24138, 3 balls; CC Celery 25773, 1 ball.

NEEDLES
US 4 (3.5 mm) straight or circular, or size to obtain gauge

NOTIONS
Tapestry Needle

GAUGE
26 sts and 30 rows = 4" in Brocade pattern, blocked.

Thistle Kitchen Towels

Notes:
These simple yet elegant kitchen towels feature a thistle motif worked at each end. Make 2 identical towels.

DIRECTIONS

With MC and using a Knitted Cast-on, CO 91 sts. Work in Garter st (Knit every row) for 5 rows. On the next (RS) row, break MC and attach CC and begin working from Thistle Border chart. On the second row of the chart, reattach MC for stranding.

After the last (RS) row of the chart, break CC and slide the work to the other end of the needle or transfer back to the left hand needle, so that you are ready to begin a RS row. With MC, work in Garter st for 6 rows.

On the next RS row, begin working from Brocade chart across all sts. Work from chart for 15", ending having completed a WS row. Work in Garter st for 6 rows.

Break MC and attach CC. Begin working from Thistle Border 2 chart, attaching MC on second row for stranding.

After the last row of the chart, break CC and slide the work to the other end of the needle or transfer back to the left hand needle, so that you are ready to begin a RS row. With MC, work in Garter st for 5 rows. BO all sts.

Finishing
Weave in ends, wash and block to finished measurements.

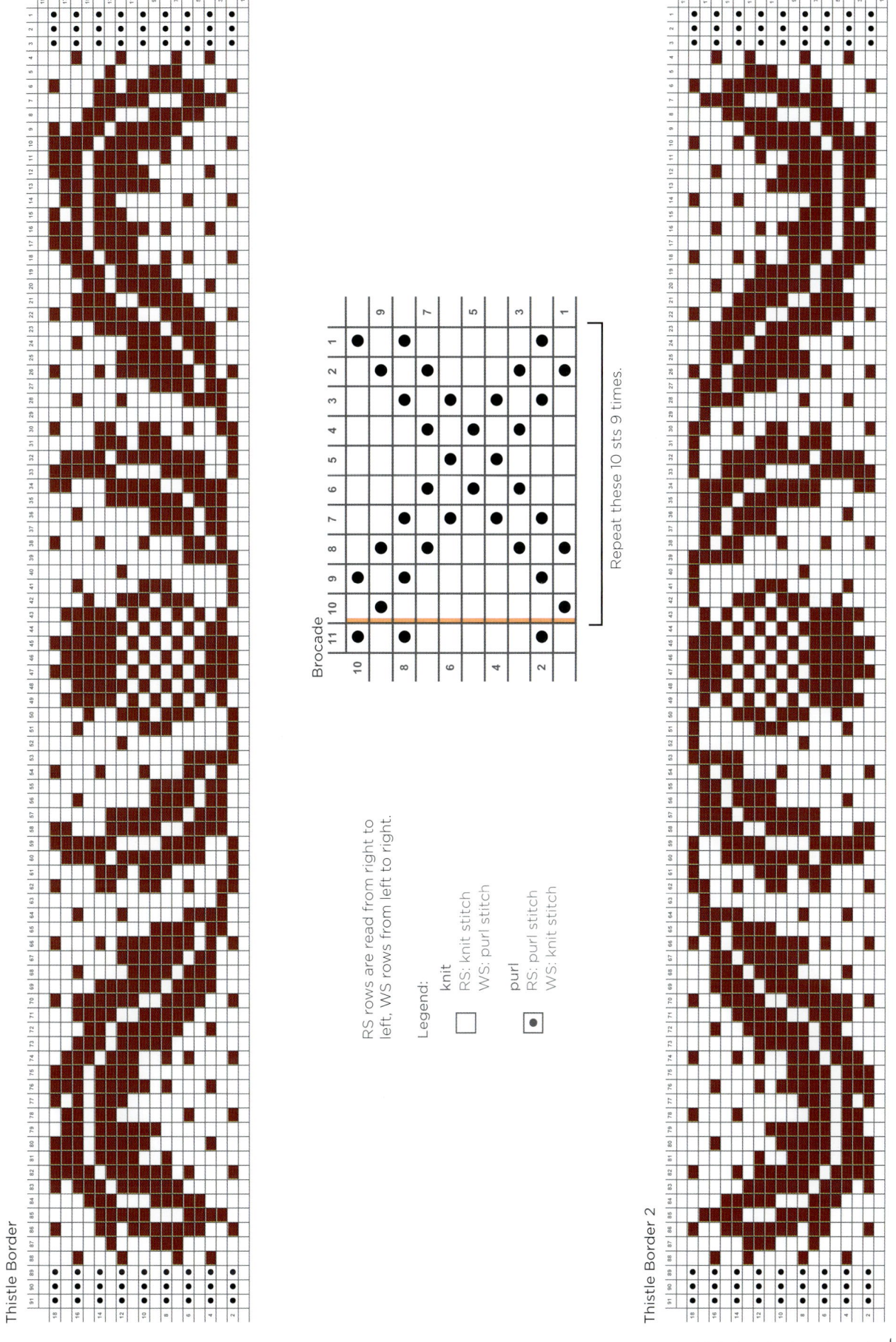

Thistle Border

Brocade

Repeat these 10 sts 9 times.

RS rows are read from right to left, WS rows from left to right.

Legend:

knit
RS: knit stitch
WS: purl stitch

purl
RS: purl stitch
WS: knit stitch

Thistle Border 2

Thistle Kitchen Towels | **23**

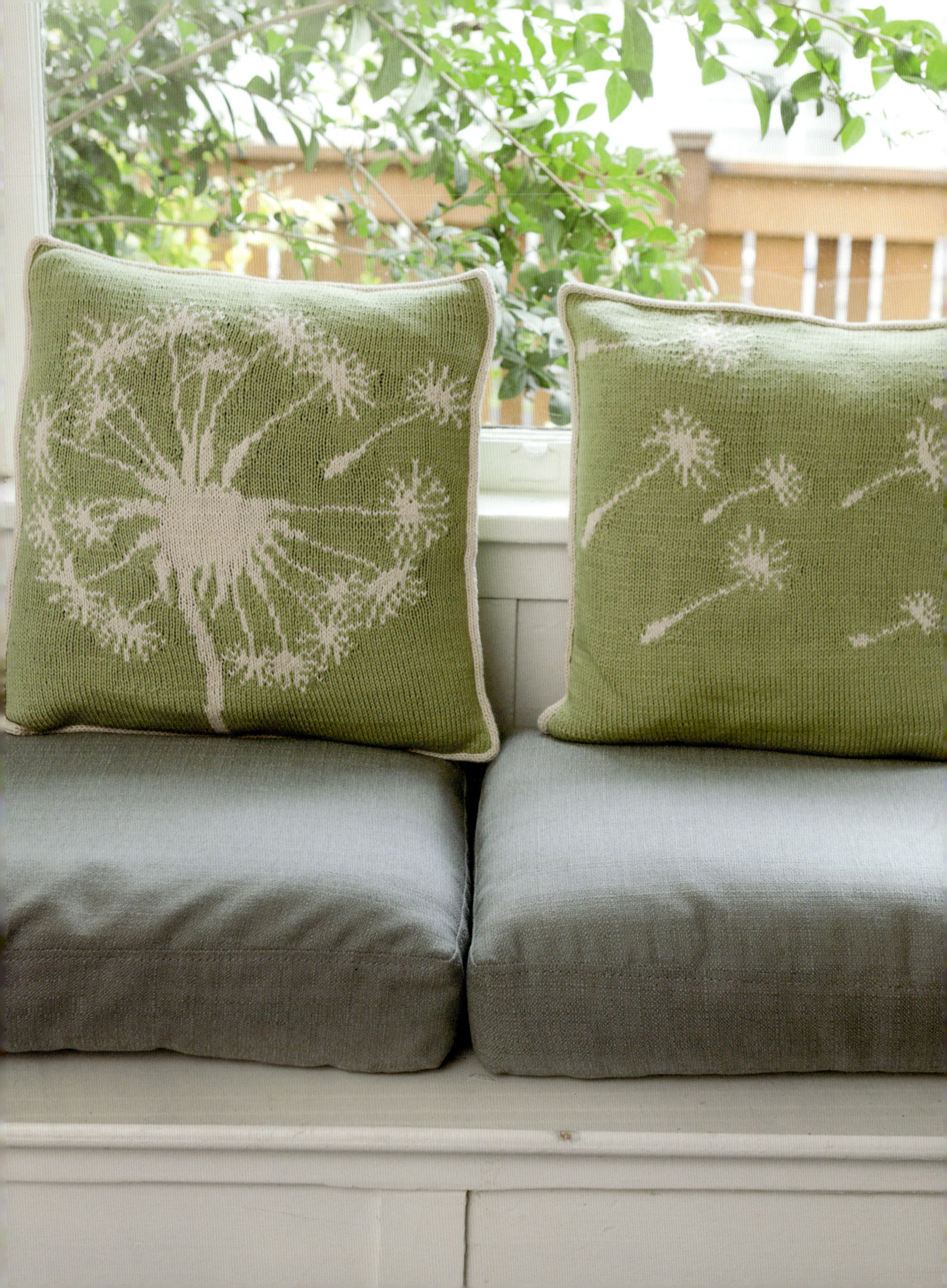

DANDELION PILLOWS

by Kerin Dimeler-Laurence

FINISHED MEASUREMENTS
16" Square

YARN
Knit Picks Comfy Sport (75% Pima Cotton, 25% Acrylic; 136 yards/50g): MC Honeydew 24425, 10 balls; CC Ivory 24429, 2 balls.

NEEDLES
US 3 (3.25mm) straight or circular needle, or size to obtain gauge
US 3 (3.25mm) DPNs for I-cord border

NOTIONS
Tapestry Needle
Two 16" Pillowforms
Eight 1.25" Buttons
Thin yarn or thread to mark I-Cord placement

GAUGE
24 sts and 33 rows = 4" in St st, blocked.

Dandelion Pillows | 25

Dandelion Pillows

Notes:
Dandelion seeds drift across this pair of pillows. Each pillow is worked flat, then joined at the top and bottom seams with I-cord. Buttons up the back keep each cover in place over the pillowform.

The Dandelion motif can be worked in a combination of stranded and Intarsia knitting, where the CC is wrapped around the MC every row at the edges of the design, but is stranded with the MC over the more detailed portions. The Seeds motifs can be worked in Intarsia or duplicate stitched on afterwards.

DIRECTIONS
With MC, CO 208 sts. Work a set-up row (RS): (K1, P1) 7 times, PM to mark edge of button band, K 42, PM to mark beginning of pattern, work from either Dandelion chart or Seeds chart over the next 96 sts, PM to mark end of pattern, K 42, PM to mark buttonhole band, (P1, K1) 7 times.

Continue working pillow as established, working the Button band and Buttonhole band in rib, the back panels in plain St st, and the front in pattern from either chart. As you work the pillow, run a thin contrasting yarn or thread up the 'ladder' where the two markers outline the front motif; this will be removed later, but will mark where the I-cord border will be worked.

At the same time, work Buttonholes.
When the pillow is 2" long, work the first Buttonhole over Buttonhole Band:
Row 1 (RS): (P1, K1) twice, P1, BO next 4 sts, (K1, P1) twice, K1.
Row 2: (P1, K1) twice, P1, CO 4 sts, (K1, P1) twice, K1.
Repeat the buttonhole every 4" three more times.

After the last row of the chart, BO all sts in MC.

I-Cord Border
An I-cord border is worked all the way around the pillows, marking the border of the front motif and joining the top and bottom of the pillow.

Place the pillowcase face down. Fold the back panels toward the center along the stitched lines, laying the Buttonhole band over the Buttonband. The bands should overlap completely. With locking ring markers, safety pins or straight pins, pin the edges in place through all layers of fabric.

With Ivory, CO 3 sts onto one DPN and begin I-cord starting at a bottom corner, ready to work across the bottom:
*Knit two stitches and slip the third stitch knitwise.
PU and knit one stitch through the edge of all layers of fabric together. You will now have 4 stitches on your right needle. Do not turn.

Use your left needle tip to pass the slipped stitch over the last knitted stitch. This will leave you with three stitches on your right needle.

Slip these three stitches back onto the left needle tip, or slide to the other end of the needle, purlwise. Tug on the working yarn to tighten up the stitches and pull the working yarn tightly across the back, creating a tube of stitches.

Repeat these steps from * across the bottom, joining the two sides together.

Work the Applied I-cord up one side of the pillow, working into the ladder between two stitches where the line of thread marks the border between front and back. Slide thread out ahead of your stitching. At the top edge, remove thread completely.

Work Applied I-cord across the top edge of the pillow the same way as done for the bottom, picking up sts through all layers and closing the edge. Work Applied I-cord down the side towards the bottom, as done for the other side.

At the corner, break yarn, leaving 6" tail. Use a tapestry needle to graft the live sts to the cast on with the yarn tail.

Finishing
Weave in ends, wash and block to finished measurements. Sew buttons opposite buttonholes. Slip each cover over a pillowform and button in place.

Dandelion

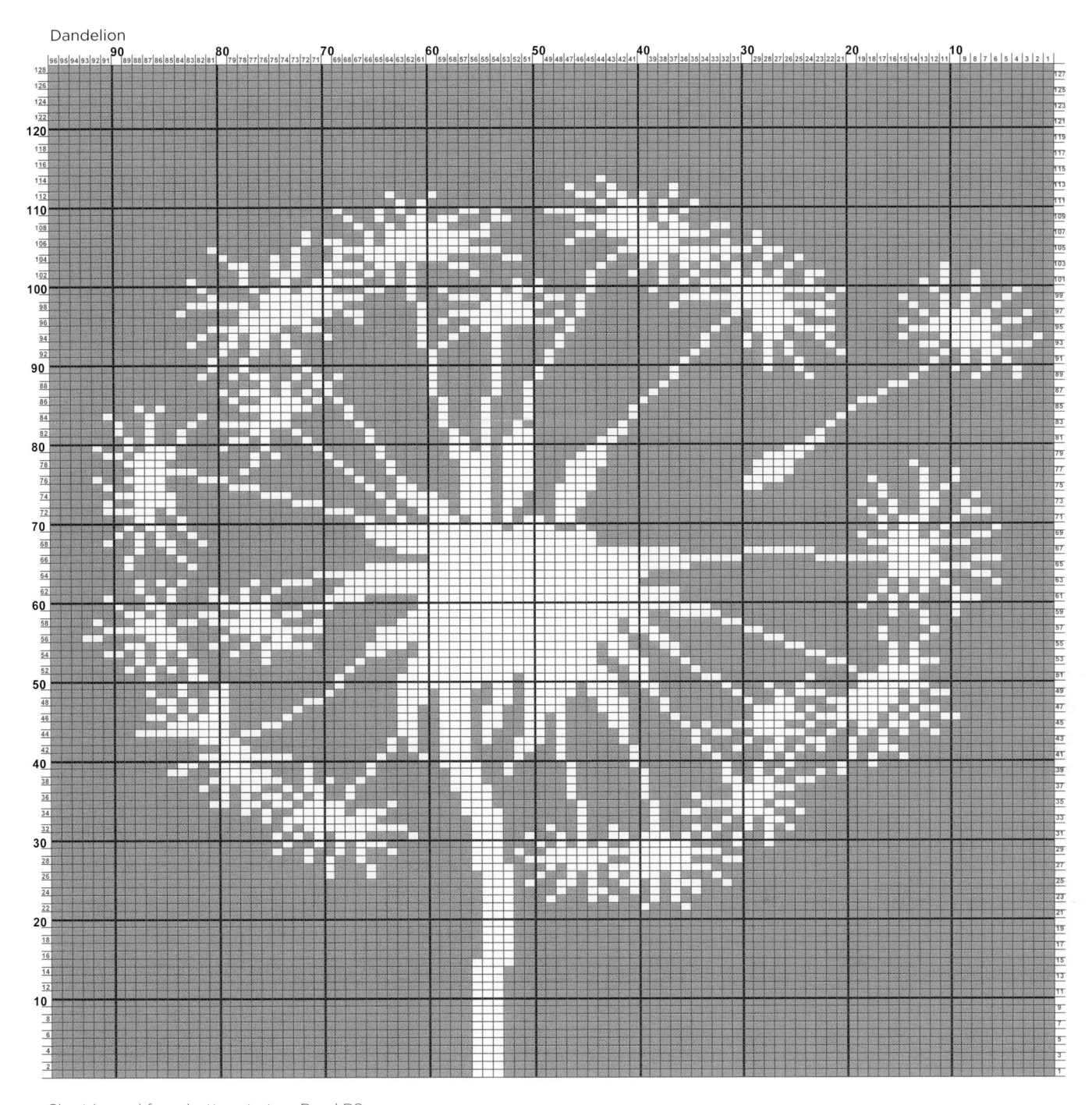

Chart is read from bottom to top. Read RS rows from right to left and WS rows from left to right.

Blue lines occur every 10 stitches and 10 rows to help you keep your place.

Dandelion Pillows | 27

28 | Dandelion Pillows

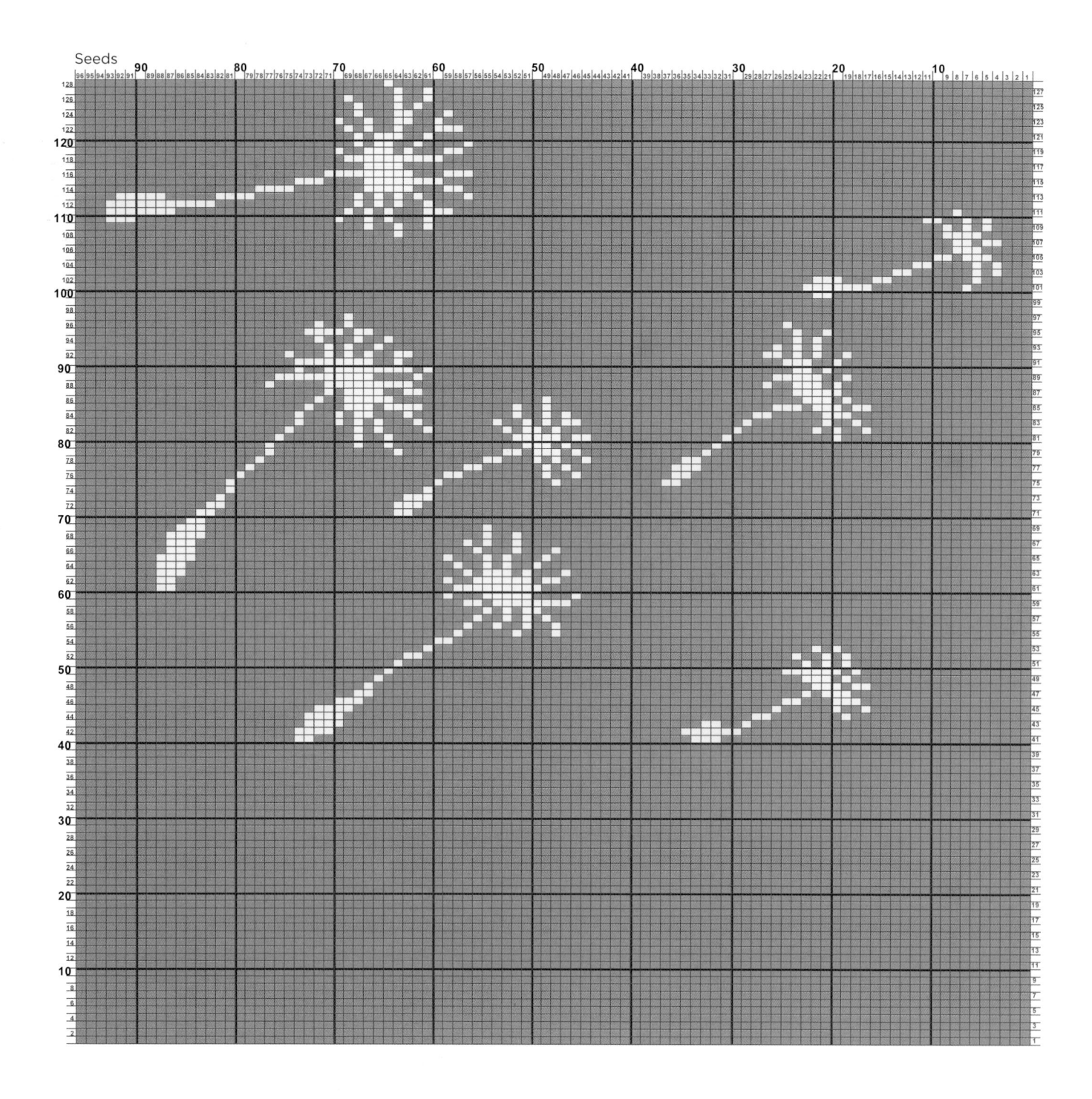

Dandelion Pillows | 29

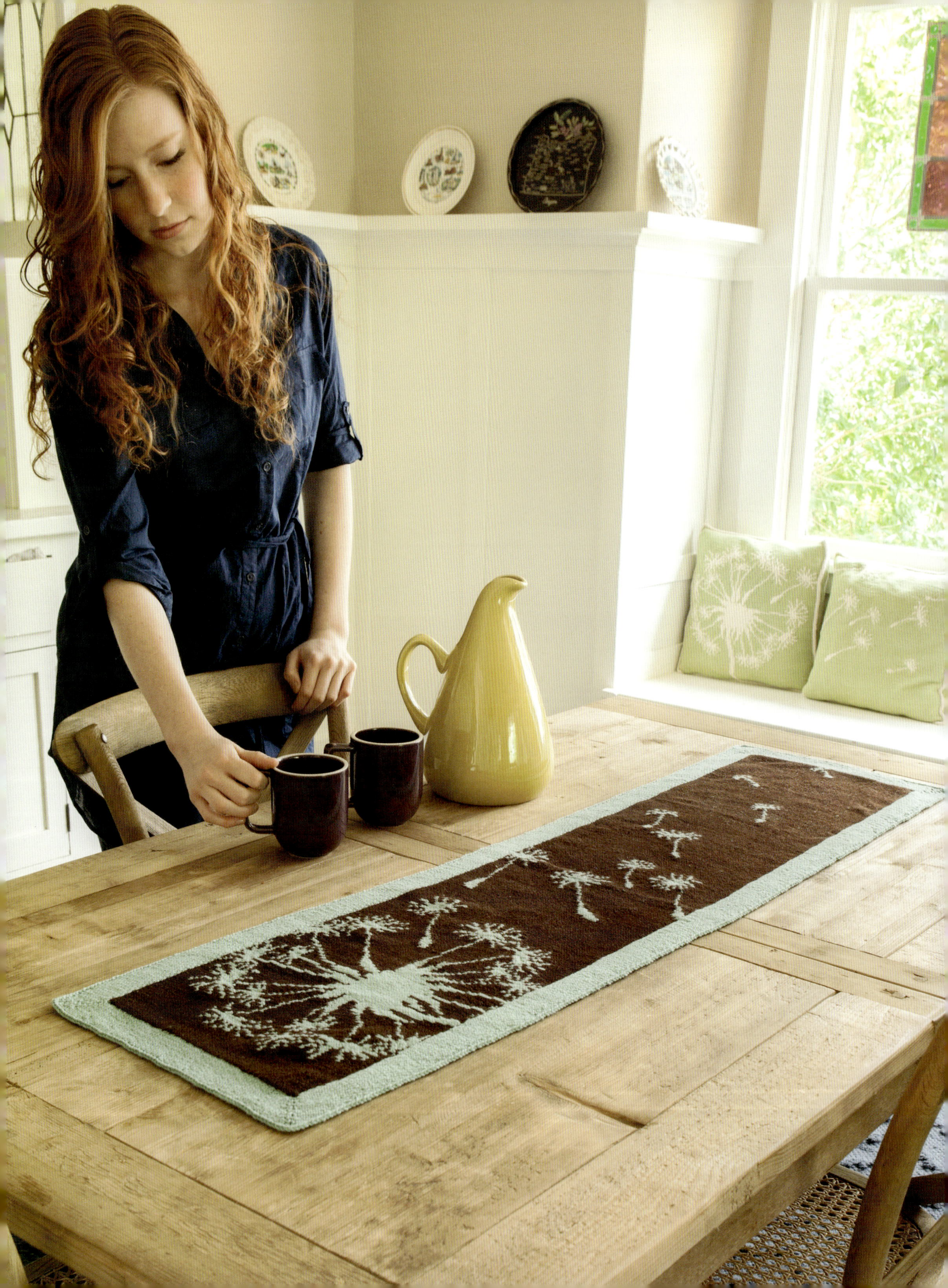

DANDELION RUNNER

by Kerin Dimeler-Laurence

FINISHED MEASUREMENTS
13x48"

YARN
Knit Picks Cotlin (70% Tanguis Cotton, 30% Linen; 123 yards/50g): MC Coffee 24138, 6 balls; CC Sagebrush 25777, 3 balls.

NEEDLES
US 4 (3.5mm) straight or circular needle, or size to obtain gauge
US 4 (3.5mm) 60" circular needle for Linen Stitch border, or size to obtain gauge

NOTIONS
Tapestry Needle
Intarsia Bonbbins (optional)

GAUGE
24 sts and 32 rows = 4" in St st, blocked.
24 sts and 48 rows = 4" in Linen St, blocked.

Dandelion Runner

Notes:
Wind-blown dandelion seeds drift by on this decorative runner.

The Dandelion motif can be worked in a combination of stranded and Intarsia knitting, where the CC is wrapped around the MC every row at the edges of the design, but is stranded with the MC over the more detailed portions. Smaller areas of color can be worked in Intarsia or duplicate stitched on afterwards.

The central motif is worked first, then stitches are picked up along the edges for a Linen Stitch border.

Mitered Linen Stitch in the round (worked over a multiple of 2 sts):
Round 1: KFB, *(Knit 1, slip 1 with yarn in front) to st before marker, KFB, SM*. Repeat between *s around: 8 sts increased.
Round 2: *Slip 1 with yarn in front, Knit 1. Repeat from * around.

DIRECTIONS

With MC, CO 272 sts. Keeping the first and last sts in MC (they will be selvedge sts for picking up), begin working from Panels 1, 2, and 3 of the Dandelion chart. After all 80 rows have been knit, BO all sts with MC.

Border

A contrasting border in Linen Stitch is picked up and worked around the central panel.

Using CC, with RS facing and starting in the lower right hand corner of Panel 1, PU and knit 60 sts up the short edge of the panel. PM, PU and K 270 sts across the top of the panel. PM, PU and K 60 sts down the left edge, PM, and PU and knit 270 sts across the bottom edge. PM and join to work in the round.

Work in Mitered Linen stitch for 18 rounds. BO all sts firmly, so that Border lays flat.

Finishing

Weave in ends, wash and block to finished measurements.

Dandelion Runner

Panel 1

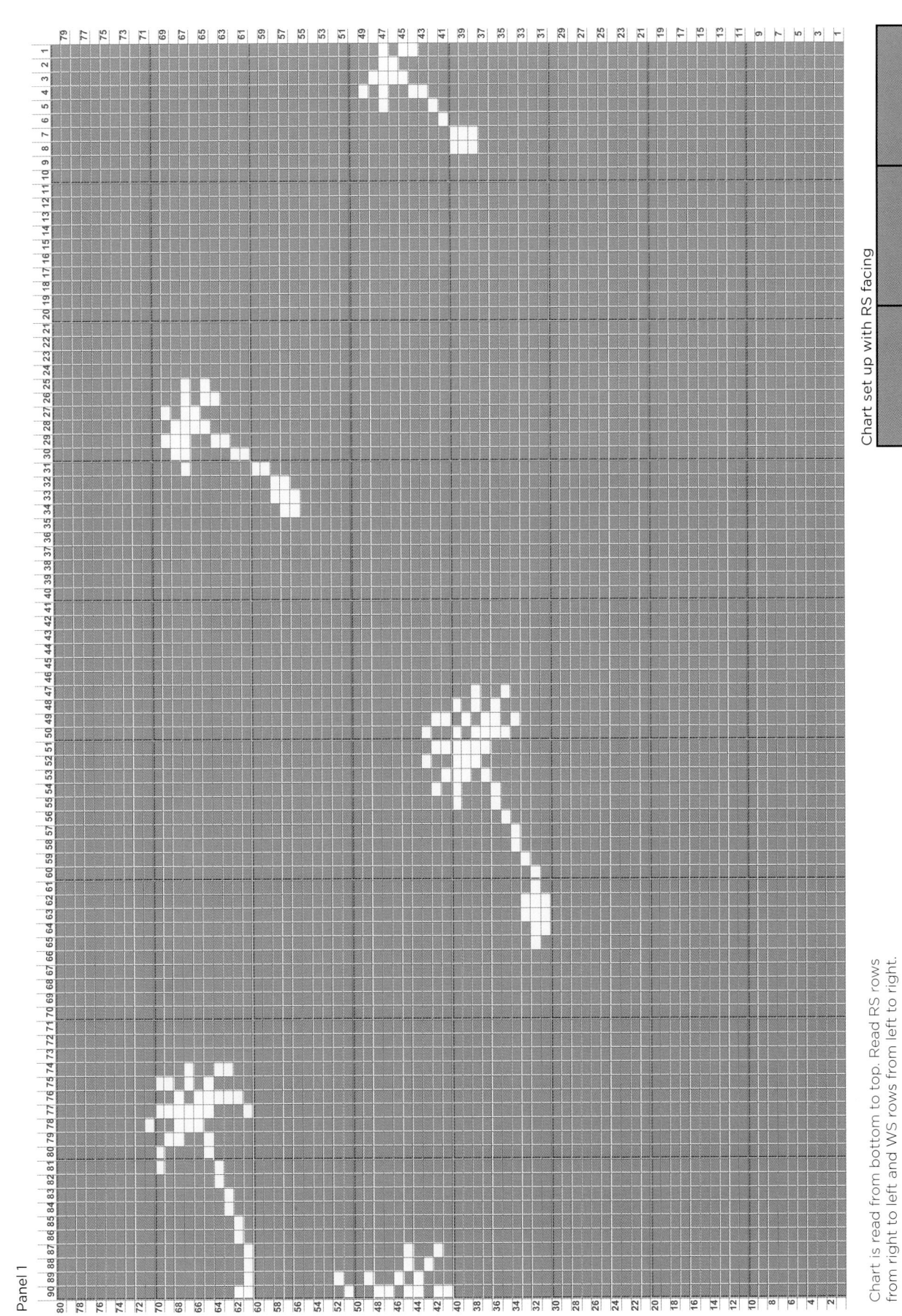

Chart set up with RS facing

Panel 1 | Panel 2 | Panel 3

Chart is read from bottom to top. Read RS rows from right to left and WS rows from left to right.

Blue lines occur every 10 stitches and 10 rows to help you keep your place.

Dandelion Runner | 33

Panel 2

34 | Dandelion Runner

Panel 3

Dandelion Runner | 35

Knit Picks

Knit Picks yarn is both luxe and affordable—a seeming contradiction trounced! But it's not just about the pretty colors; we also care deeply about fiber quality and fair labor practices, leaving you with a gorgeously reliable product you'll turn to time and time again.

This collection features

Comfy
Worsted Weight
75% Pima Cotton, 25% Acrylic

CotLin
DK Weight
70% Tanguis Cotton, 30% Linen

Dishie
Worsted Weight
100% Cotton

Comfy
Sport Weight
75% Pima Cotton, 25% Acrylic

View these beautiful yarns and more at www.KnitPicks.com